To Love and to Cherish

A GUIDE TO NON-RELIGIOUS WEDDING CEREMONIES

by Jane Wynne Willson

BRITISH HUMANIST ASSOCIATION

The British Humanist Association is a registered charity which promotes the recognition and practice of Humanist ideals and values. Free from the constraints and illusions of religious belief, we look to fellow men and women for fulfilment and mutual support. Humanists feel responsibility and concern towards all human beings, and it is in human nature that we find the roots of our morality.

Caring relationships, involving love and long-term commitment, form a integral part of the society we would like to achieve.

In the same series:

Funerals Without God: a practical guide to non-religious ceremonies (British Humanist Association 1989)

First published 1988 by the British Humanist Association, 13 Prince of Wales Terrace, London W8 5PG. Second Edition 1989

Printed and Typeset by RAP Ltd, 201 Spotland Road, Rochdale OL12 7AF.

British Library Cataloguing In Publication Data

   Willson, Jane Wynne
   To love and to cherish: a guide to non-religious wedding ceremonies
   1. Wedding customs
   I. Title II. British Humanist Association
   3921.5

ISBN 0-901825-11-5

To Love and to Cherish

Contents

Foreword

There are in Britain a great many thoughtful people who have ideals and aspirations that owe nothing to religious affiliation, who want to enter into committed marital relationships with a public ceremony to mark the rite of passage. But they feel uneasy at the thought of going through a religious one, which implies they have beliefs they do not in fact hold, or through a Registrar's, which offers no satisfying emotional or personal content.

For them, Jane Wynne Willson's book is the perfect answer. It is exactly the book these people have needed for a very long time. And they are not necessarily card-carrying Humanists!

There is meat here for all shades of belief and attitudes, short, of course, of the rigid dogmatism from which Humanism is an escape. The person who does not find here a way to mark so important a step as marriage, that will be both personal and important, will be unusual indeed.

I wish the book every success, but, perhaps more importantly, success and happiness to those who use it.

Claire Rayner

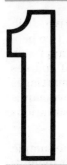

1 INTRODUCTION

Wedding Bells?

In Britain today the proportion of marriages that take place in church is about half of the total. Of these we do not know how many are the weddings of non-believers, but we can hazard a guess that the number is high. The idea of "walking up the aisle", the aura that surrounds a traditional church wedding, its solemnity and splendour, the surroundings that are usually impressive and often beautiful — all this is an understandable attraction to a great many people.

But, on the other hand, to take part in an overtly religious ceremony is likely to be an uncomfortable if not distasteful experience for those who do not believe in God. Many of the promises that are made and the sentiments that are uttered will be of immense significance to Christians, but are quite meaningless to others. They want to express a serious and important commitment, which is based on a fundamentally different view of the world.

In contrast to a church wedding, the civil marriage in a register office is found by many to be rather austere and uninspiring. It uses a form of words which must be adhered to, and these words must be acceptable to all. Thus it has to be "secular" in the sense which excludes all reference to fundamental beliefs and values. Individual expressions of commitment cannot be accommodated, though minor additions may be made at the registrar's discretion.

The Need For Ceremony

Throughout history, ceremonies have been used to mark important events in people's lives, and many of us find that a formal occasion of this kind can be very helpful. At a Humanist wedding the participants have the opportunity to declare publicly their love for each other and their aspirations for the future. They can make this commitment among their family and friends in a significant and meaningful ceremony.

The Humanist concept of a wedding ceremony is quite distinctive. It illuminates important values and beliefs while giving expression to two people's personalities. Moreover there is a flexibility and openness of approach that is quite unusual. Remarriage after divorce, the marriage of couples who already have children or where the woman is pregnant, marriages where the couple do not wish to exchange rings or where the woman is anxious to keep her own name — all kinds of unconventional situations can be accommodated.

As can be seen in the variety of sentiments that are uttered in the sample ceremonies that follow, the participants are free to describe their feelings and aspirations. They can, if they wish, use their own words to compose a ceremony that will reflect their particular concept of a Humanist marriage. It will have a flavour that is personal to them and will be totally sincere.

What Choices Do You Have?

The current legal position is extremely unsatisfactory. It discriminates against those whose beliefs do not include worship of a god. Many of us would like a real and meaningful ceremony which includes registration and is recognised by law. This, as things stand, is only possible if an authorised celebrant is prepared to perform a non-religious ceremony in a building licensed for the celebration of marriage. Only places of worship can be so licensed, and occasions like that described above are not common.

So what usually happens is that you are left with the following choices:

A Register Office Wedding

- A civil wedding at a Register Office, and no more.

A Church Wedding

- You may decide to go through with a church wedding, perhaps to please a conventionally religious family, or indeed to achieve the setting that you would like.

A Humanist Wedding

You may decide to have a ceremony of a kind used by Humanists. Then there are various alternatives before you:

- A Humanist wedding ceremony, registered at the time. With the law as it is, this may well not be possible for you.

- A Humanist ceremony, which follows a civil marriage at a Register Office.

- A Humanist ceremony before your family and friends, without legal recognition in any form.

A Change In The Law?

The law has been recently under review as part of a general efficiency drive, and various proposals have been put forward for streamlining the system. We feel there is a strong case for new legislation since the present law discriminates so unnecessarily against those outside the churches. What is needed is a system whereby suitable individuals are given the necessary authority to perform wedding ceremonies and there is a reasonable choice of places where weddings may be held. Such arrangements as this work satisfactorily in Australia and New Zealand.

Meanwhile the number of requests for help with Humanist wedding ceremonies, either by providing celebrants, or suggesting material for people to use, continues to rise. This short booklet is our attempt to help meet this demand and to give some food for thought to those considering marriage.

 # FOUR SAMPLE CEREMONIES

The following pages contain the texts of four ceremonies that have been used during the past few years. Apart from the American ceremony, which is a somewhat shorter version of the original, the texts are faithfully reproduced. Each has a different flavour and the collection will, we hope, give an idea of the wide variety of style that can be used.

First Ceremony

This ceremony is based on the form of words used for many years by the South Place Ethical Society in London. This wedding was conducted in a university chapel by a broad minded chaplain, and was registered and thus legally valid. All the music was live.

(J.S. Bach "Sonata in G minor")

We come here together to witness the joining of two lives. In the words of Shakespeare's sonnet:

"Let me not to the marriage of true minds
Admit impediments. Love is not love
Which alters when it alteration finds,
Or bends with the remover to remove:
O, no! — it is an ever-fixed mark,
That looks on tempests and is never shaken.
It is the star to every wandering barque,
Whose worth's unknown, although its height be taken.
Love's not Time's fool, though rosy lips and cheeks
Within his bending sickle's compass come;
Love alters not with his brief hours and weeks,
But bears it out even to the edge of doom.
If this be error, and upon me proved.
I never writ, nor no man ever loved."

Mark and Helena have come here in affection and honour to say before us that they will henceforth share their home, combine in mutual living and responsibility and give their joint support to the life of the community. Love is the wish of the whole self to unite with another to the end of personal completeness. Touched by this love, nature yields tenderness, togetherness, simplicity, honesty and delight. When a man and a woman openly and sincerely declare their affection for each other they are affirming the precious truth that love is the foundation of all life — between men and women, between parents and children, between friends and, as goodwill, between all mankind. Hence we are present here as witness not only to a legal act but also to a deeper truth.

(Helena and Mark stand)

CELEBRANT: In the name of the community we represent, we ask this man and this woman to speak in truth to one another and to repeat in the spirit of faithful engagement these words of solemn declaration that bind them together:

Will you, Mark, say after me: "I do solemnly declare / that I know not of any lawful impediment / why I, Mark (surname), / may not be joined in matrimony / to Helena (surname)."*

Will you, Helena, say after me: "I do solemnly declare / that I know not of any lawful impediment / why I, Helena (surname), / may not be joined in matrimony / to Mark (surname)."*

Will you join your right hands.

Will you, Mark, repeat after me: "I call upon these persons here present / to witness that I, Mark (surname), / take thee, Helena (surname), / to be my lawful wedded wife."*

Will you, Helena, repeat after me: "I call upon these persons here present / to witness that I, Helena (surname), / take thee, Mark (surname), / to be my lawful wedded husband."*

Now, together, repeat after me these words:

"We have wed each other / and do pledge ourselves in honour / to prefer each other's good / and to work together for the common good. / We aspire to have and to hold together / from this day forwards / for better or for worse / for richer or for poorer / in sickness and in health / and to love and to cherish / as long as we may live."

I pronounce you husband and wife.

(Signing of the register — Ravel "Pavane".)
Now we all offer to you, Helena, and you, Mark, our heartfelt good wishes. May you have joy and give joy, and make your home a source of strength

and happiness. May you rest in each other's love, affection and delight and enjoy marriage as the supreme embodiment of your nature. Be happy and see that your happiness overflows to others. Two people secure to each other the enjoyment of their most personal needs. In marriage we are uniquely enabled to be ourselves, and to know one another, to share each other's troubles and to appreciate each other's diversities. Marriage and family combine an institution with the grace and individuality of a personal relationship.

In the name of this community I wish you both all the joy and happiness that mutual love can bring. Look forward confidently to a future in which you and the world in which you live and work will be the better and the happier for this joyful occasion.

(Handel "Allegro from Sonata in F")

Second Ceremony

This is an American Humanist marriage ceremony written by Corliss Lamont. It has been slightly abbreviated and the names of the participants altered, but is otherwise unchanged.

CELEBRANT: Sam and Marilyn have come to love each other deeply and sincerely. They now wish to unite their lives and establish a home together. In this ceremony they dedicate themselves to the happiness and well-being of each other. Marriage is a sharing of experience and an adventure in the most intimate of human relationships. It is the joyous union of a man and a woman whose comradeship and mutual understanding have flowered into love. Here today Sam and Marilyn proclaim that love to the world, and we who are gathered here rejoice with them and for them in the new life they now undertake together.

Sam and Marilyn have chosen to be married in this Humanist wedding ceremony. Humanism sees a human being as an active and inseparable unity of body and personality. Reason is the guide, but reason never separated from the emotions and strivings of the whole person; so that emotion and intellect functioning together provide the firmest foundation for married love. Sam and Marilyn hold in common the interests and ideals of a Humanist world. Living together in this way, they will deepen their love for each other and extend its reach to their fellow Humanists and to the whole community of humankind.

It is a Humanist belief that there should be equality between men and women in every relevant way, and that it is especially important for this principle to be recognised in the marriage relationship. Humanists repudiate the old tradition of the wife who meekly obeys her husband. Marriage must be a cooperative venture. It is a relationship based on love, respect, and a determination on the part of both wife and husband to adjust to each other's temperaments and moods — in health or sickness, joy or sadness, ease or hardship. The marriage of Sam and Marilyn means the creation of a new home and family. The family has continued to show great hardihood as an institution and thrives throughout the world. In an age when many traditional values have crumbled it becomes all the more important to recognise the significance of devoted and affectionate family life.

(The bridge and groom now stand)

CELEBRANT: Sam, will you have Marilyn to be your wedded wife, to share your life with her, and do you pledge that you will love, honour and tenderly care for her in all the varying circumstances of your lives?

GROOM: I will.

CELEBRANT: Marilyn, will you have this man to be your wedded husband, to share your life with him, and do you pledge that you will love, honour and care for him in tenderness and affection through all the varying experiences of your lives?

BRIDE: I will.

(The bride and groom now address each other)

GROOM: Marilyn, I acknowledge my love and respect for you and invite you to share my life as I hope to share yours. I promise to recognise you as an equal individual at all times, and to be conscious of your development as well as my own. I shall seek through kindness and understanding to achieve with you the life we have envisioned. In token of my love and devotion, I place this ring on your finger.

BRIDE: Sam, I acknowledge my love and respect for you and invite you to share my life as I hope to share yours. I promise to recognise you as an equal individual at all times, and to be conscious of your development as well as my own. I shall seek through kindness and understanding to achieve with you the life we have envisioned. In token of my love and devotion, I place this ring on your finger.

CELEBRANT: Inasmuch as Sam and Marilyn have consented together in this ceremony to live in wedlock and have witnessed their undertaking in the presence of this company by the giving and receiving of rings, I now pronounce that they are husband and wife.

To celebrate the event we will now read these lines from an American Indian ceremony:

"Now you will feel no rain, for each of you will be shelter for the other. Now you will feel no cold, for each of you will be warmth to the other. Now there is no more loneliness.
Now you are two persons, but there is only one life before you.
Go now to your dwelling to enter into the days of your life together.
And may your days be good and long upon the earth."

Third Ceremony

This was a private ceremony, for two people who had both been married before. It was held at home and conducted by a friend in front of invited friends and relations. It was followed by a legal name change the following day at a solicitor's office, where a certificate was issued.

FRIEND: Those of us who have experienced the impermanence of marriage by whatever cause, are forced to reconsider the nature of this institution. Some seek to state vows before their God and some make a commitment before an official of the State. Janet and Roland have chosen a third way, that of making a declaration in the presence of some of those whom they love and whose friendship they enjoy. They wish to declare their commitment to one another and their hope that this will be a loving relationship for as long as they live. For them marriage is not primarily concerned with property or similar rights but with their intention to love and support each other and their families. It is such a marriage that is celebrated for them today. By being here and sharing in this occasion, you help to give reality and significance to their marriage.

JANET: In acknowledging our love and respect for each other as equal individuals, I affirm my desire to make a life together in mutual support for the rest of our lives. I give you this ring as a symbol of my love.

ROLAND: In acknowledging our love and respect for each other as equal individuals, I affirm my desire to make a life together in mutual support for the rest of our lives. I give you this ring as a symbol of my love.

Fourth Ceremony

Like the first ceremony this was held in a university chapel and was legally valid. It was unconventional in that the couple already had two children. Apart from the two sections which are legal requirements (these are marked

with asterisks), the wording was written by them for the occasion. All the music was live.
(John Field "Marche Triomphale")

CELEBRANT: We come here today to celebrate the joining of two lives. Ruth and Steve have decided to mark their relationship and give public recognition to it. They have written this ceremony themselves and, apart from two passages which are legal requirements, it has been composed specially for the occasion. They felt that, by writing something new rather than adapting the traditional wedding service, they could highlight the similarities rather than the differences between their beliefs and those of some of their family and friends. We will begin by singing together a song about an experience we can all share — the appreciation of natural beauty.

ALL: A Day In Autumn
(see section on Music)

The commitment that Ruth and Steve express to each other today in front of their family and friends is not new, but has been built up gradually over the eight years they have known each other. They feel that the time has come to look at their relationship and to define to each other and explain to us their vision of their future together. Anatole France wrote: "It is not enough to love passionately; you must also love well. A passionate love is good doubtless, but a beautiful love is better. May you have as much strength as gentleness; may it lack nothing, not even forbearance, and let even a little compassion be mingled with it ... You are human, and because of this capable of much suffering. If then something of compassion does not enter into the feelings you have one for the other, these feelings will not always befit all the circumstances of your life together; they will be like festive robes that will not shield you from wind and rain. We love truly only those we love even in their weakness and their poverty. To forbear, to forgive, to console, that alone is the science of love."

(Music: Balcony and Marriage Scenes from West Side Story)

CELEBRANT: Ruth and Steve believe that love in its many forms is the foundation of all life; between friends, between lovers, between parents and children, between sisters and brothers and among all humankind. We are present here as witness not only to a legal act but to a deeper truth.

(Ruth and Steve stand)

In the name of the community we represent, we ask Ruth and Steve to speak to each other these words of solemn declaration.

RUTH: I do solemnly declare that I know not of any lawful impediment why I, Ruth (surname), may not be joined in matrimony to Steven (surname).*

STEVE: I do solemnly declare that I know not of any lawful impediment why I, Steven (surname), may not be joined in matrimony to Ruth (surname).*

CELEBRANT: Will you join your right hands.

RUTH: I call upon these persons here present to witness that I, Ruth (surname), do take thee, Steven (surname), to be my lawful wedded husband.*

STEVE: I call upon these persons here present to witness that I, Steven (surname), do take thee, Ruth (surname), to be my lawful wedded wife.*

CELEBRANT: Ruth and Steve, do you aspire to love each other and to live together in a spirit of tolerance, mutual support and concern for each other's well-being, sharing your responsibilities, your problems and your joys?

RUTH and STEVE: Yes, we do.

Do you aspire to help each other to provide a loving and stable home for your children; to cooperate in bringing them up to be caring, honest and happy people?

RUTH and STEVE: Yes, we do.

Do you aspire to work together for the welfare of the community to which you and your family belong, and to share with each other a wider concern for humanity?

RUTH and STEVE: Yes, we do.

I pronounce you husband and wife.

(Music while the marriage register is being signed)

Now we all wish you fulfilment in your lives together and success in working towards your ideals. We hope you will be happy and that you will be able to make your home a source of strength to your children, family and friends. We will end by singing together a song which looks forward to a happy future.

ALL: "Ode to Joy"

(see Section on Music).

(Chopin "Polonaise in A Major", as people leave the ceremony.)

 # THE PRACTICAL SIDE

There are three quite separate parts of the job ahead, if you are planning a Humanist wedding ceremony:-

- finding someone to act as celebrant.
- composing the form of words, choosing the music etc.
- organising details of time and place, including arrangements for a reception, if any.

In both the first and second of these help may be sought from the British Humanist Association (whose address is given at the back of this booklet.) But the practical arrangements and hard work involved in the third are not the concern of the BHA, whose celebrants are likely to be busy people, though they will gladly give up their time to help with music and words.

Finding A Celebrant

There are a number of possibilities here. As in our third ceremony, you may have a friend who would be happy to perform the role for you. You may decide to approach the BHA or your local Humanist group for help, or ask some Humanist whom you happen to know. You may have access to a college or university chapel, where one of the chaplains would be prepared to conduct a non-religious wedding ceremony. Or a Unitarian minister might be happy to do this. In these last two instances the marriage will of course be legally valid. A lot depends on the sort of place and the kind of atmosphere you would prefer.

Who Does What?

Whoever the celebrant may be, it is essential to be absolutely clear exactly what you are asking them to do. As was pointed out above, this should be limited to help and advice with composing the form of words to be used, and with conducting the actual ceremony.

If the celebrant is a personal friend there will obviously be no fee involved. If he or she is a chaplain there will be a fixed amount to pay. A BHA celebrant, or one from a local group, will be glad to receive a similar fee.

Writing Your Own Words

There is no set formula for people to follow in devising their own ceremony. The celebrant will be ready to offer suggestions and help with the wording if this is needed. The couple will want to pick their own poetry and music: we hope they will find the notes at the end of this booklet helpful. There are likely to be some who will follow closely an established form, while others will prefer to write the whole thing themselves.

A Useful Framework

It can be seen from the sample texts that, though there is much variety of content and style, they all share a basic structure. The ceremony tends to fall naturally into five parts:-

- Entry (usually to music.)
- Celebrant welcomes everyone, introduces the couple and makes a few opening remarks.
- Celebrant continues with general comments on the Humanist concept of marriage (see Chap. 4); the particular circumstances of this occasion; the couple's own thoughts and feelings about themselves and their partnership. This can be followed by the reading of a poem or a passage of prose that is particularly appropriate, by music or by singing.
- THE MARRIAGE. (The bride and groom stand.) This is the important part of the ceremony, and the moment when the participants state their aspirations to each other in front of those of their family and friends who are present. If the occasion is one that will qualify as a legal act, there are two parts that are obligatory, and these are marked with asterisks in the first and fourth ceremonies. If it is a private occasion, which may or may not be preceded by registration, then the choice of words is for the couple to decide. But it must be emphasised that, even if the event is not one that will be legally recognised, the actual marriage words will constitute the meaningful part of the ceremony to all those present, and should be included. At the end of this section the celebrant declares that the couple are now man and wife. Again, this may or may not be the case in law, but certainly is so in the eyes of the assembled company.
- Closing words, good wishes etc. Exit to music.

Checklist Of Things To Be Done

There are countless things to be done. Notice must be given at your local Register Office if the marriage is to be legalised. If this is done well in advance (ie. 22 days or more before the legalisation of the wedding) there need be no licence and the cost will be less. Even in the case of a "wedding by licence" there must be a lapse of one week, or a wedding with legal standing cannot take place.

The couple must decide on the place, date and time for the ceremony at the earliest possible stage, and agree this with the celebrant.

It is their job to see that the room or hall is appropriate to the number of people they plan to invite; to decide on the venue for the reception and the catering arrangements; to choose ushers, if there are to be any, and brief them thoroughly.

They will be wise to arrange a rehearsal the day before the wedding, at which everyone directly involved is present, so that the seating arrangements and the exact positions for the bride, groom and celebrant can be finalised. The precise timing, from the arrival of the first guest to the moment the newly-weds leave the room, must be agreed.

If it is thought desirable for everyone present to sign a book as a record of the occasion, this will need to be organised.

If access to the room or hall is needed before the ceremony, for flower arrangement, moving chairs or setting up tape recorders, the caretaker must be consulted and briefed well in advance.

The preparations for a wedding are manifold and apply to a large extent whether the wedding is a religious one or not. Possibly the best place to look for practical help is in a current issue of a bridal magazine such as "Brides", which publishes a comprehensive wedding guide.

4 WHAT'S IT ALL ABOUT?

A Humanist View Of Marriage

Those for whom the concept of a non-religious ceremony is quite new, and those who are meeting Humanist ideas for the first time, will naturally wish to have some explanation of our views on marriage. This chapter does not claim to speak for every individual Humanist, but sets out some fundamental points on which the majority of us would be in agreement.

In this booklet we have already mentioned "marriage" a number of times. We have been referring to the long-term commitment between two adults that for many will be embodied in a registered marriage. But most of what we say will be equally relevant to any two adults who wish to commit themselves to a long-term relationship, whether acknowledged by law or not, including partners of the same sex. Our concern in this chapter is the human relationship, not its legal status.

Humanists look on marriage as a commitment that involves mutual love and respect. Each party has a responsibility for the welfare of the other, and to the success of the relationship. Where a couple have children the commitment involves a shared responsibility for their well-being and development.

Choosing The Right Partner

We see marriage as important for family life and for society. Obviously adults who are happy and fulfilled in their relationships generate stability and happiness. So, in any long-term partnership, mutual compatibility is of the utmost importance. A stable and happy relationship is not likely to grow from an immature or impulsive choice of partner, perhaps made in the first flush of romantic love. For it seems sadly clear that mutual physical attraction on its own is not enough to survive the stresses of a long marriage.

We think it can show wisdom and forethought for a couple to live together and get to know each other well, before embarking on a long-term commitment. Premarital relationships, which may or may not include sex, should give the people concerned the opportunity to reach a fuller awareness of their own needs and emotions, and to develop a greater sensitivity to their partner's feelings. But we recognise that this arrangement will not suit everyone, and we are not prepared to lay down hard and fast rules of conduct.

Humanists regard physical love as one of the greatest of human joys; we believe that people should "make love" in a natural, open and responsible way. For, with modern contraception, love can be expressed freely, without fear of pregnancy. Unfortunately in this country we have inherited from our Christian culture views on sexual matters that are riddled with guilt and misunderstandings. We consider that such attitudes have caused much unhappiness and suffering in the past. The way individuals express their sexuality is a matter for them alone, **so long as** they act with mutual love and consideration. We abhor force, violence and degradation.

We believe that the sense of responsibility that underpins all Humanist morality is particularly important in sexual morality. We encourage an open and healthy attitude to sex although, in the post AIDS era, we cannot condone a multiplicity of partners. We seek to avoid, so far as we can, hurting those who are close to us as well as other people.

Settling Down

Our enthusiasm should not be taken to imply that we are advocating marriage for everyone. Of course not. Though it will be the ultimate culmination for many, others will be happier remaining single, and prefer not to embark on such a long-term commitment.

If a couple do decide to settle down, they may choose to mark the occasion with a wedding ceremony, or they may not. Often the decision to marry is made when they plan to start a family, but by no means always. Many couples are unable to have children, many do not want children: this is their private concern.

For those who choose to mark the occasion with a wedding ceremony, a few characteristics of a Humanist marriage are worth noting, for they are reflected in the ceremony itself.

- Humanists do not normally express "vows" but "aspirations". We state our firm hope and intention of achieving our aims and honouring our commitments. At the same time we think we are realistic and honest enough to recognise that these aspirations may not in fact be realised in the long term, as people and circumstances change.

- The man and the woman enjoy equal status in a Humanist marriage.
- The couple are likely to look beyond themselves and their family and express a wider concern for humanity.

Home and Family

The creation of the next generation is, for Humanists, of supreme importance. Having no belief in immortality, our challenge is to leave behind a better world for future generations everywhere; and a couple with children have a special responsibility here. Parenthood should not be undertaken in a casual or haphazard way and children should only be planned when parents are prepared to devote themselves to their upbringing. They must also be able to provide the necessary support and care for their children until they become independent, although there will be different ways of achieving this.

Humanists are concerned that present social stereotyping still imposes serious bias against the freedoms of the mother. In a family with children we would encourage the father to stay at home while the mother goes out to work, where this suits the **actual** abilities and preferences of both parties. When both parents are in the same line of work, a system of job-sharing can be an excellent solution.

Companionship

It is important that the necessary emphasis on the responsibilities of parenthood does not obscure the depth of Humanist concern with that long-term commitment which we are here calling "marriage". The close and loving relationship of two human beings that is the central feature of marriage lies right at the heart of Humanism. Those who do not believe in a god depend on their fellow humans to an even greater extent for support and fulfilment. In this closest of unions people can find a companionship and a sharing of experience that is unique. In an ideal world, companionship, mutual love and sexual fulfilment would continue until old age, and for some couples this does happen. For many, the familiarity of living together and the years of shared experience give security and comfort. Deep affection and mature love are an additional bonus for the fortunate — or perhaps the wise! Where the marriage does break down, the people involved will suffer as much distress as others. But our natural feelings of failure, and possibly guilt, will arise from the hurt we have inflicted and our inability to fulfil our aspirations and intentions. It will not derive from our failure to honour vows which we made before "God".

So Humanist marriage offers a wide spectrum of choice, to suit the aspirations and temperaments of individual couples. Yet underpinning it all are the central tenets of serious commitment, mutual concern and shared responsibility.

5 MUSIC FOR WEDDING CEREMONIES

The choice of music for a Humanist wedding ceremony is so clearly a matter of personal taste, that it would be inappropriate to make a lot of suggestions here. As the ceremony is likely to be unconventional, music of any kind can suitably be played. Jazz, folk, pop, light classical, Country and Western, songs from films or musicals, love songs ... whatever is right for the particular couple is right for the occasion. There is no reason at all to stick with classical music, unless you want to.

Some people may be in a position to organise live music; the majority will probably have to opt for some form of recording. In either event it will be necessary to discover what facilities there are in the hall or room, and what equipment will need importing.

For those who prefer a more traditional atmosphere, there can be no objection to using one of the famous Wedding Marches, as they have no religious associations. Those by Mendelssohn (from "A Midsummer Night's Dream") and by Wagner ("Here Comes the Bride") are the best known examples.

It must be borne in mind that a proportion of those present at most weddings are likely to be religious, or at least conventional. So the couple may want to include some music that will be familiar to them. For this reason, and because singing together to a familiar tune can be an enjoyable and moving experience, couples often include some communal singing in their ceremony. Everyone knows how dreary such singing can be if the assembled company knows neither the tune nor the words. What is needed is a familiar tune and words that express congenial ideas and feelings.

We are including details of three such songs, as they are not easy to find; all of them have been used recently in this way. Of these the first, Ben Jonson's love song, is sung to the traditional folk tune. The "Ode to Joy" comes from the finale of Beethoven's Ninth Symphony; the words given here are not a translation of those that Beethoven used (which refer to God) but are from a collection entitled "Social Worship", published by the London Ethical Societies in 1913. Our third example has words from the same source, but the tune of Richmond is commonly sung by Christians to the words "There is a green hill far away". A reasonable number of people in this country would be able to join in singing any of these three songs, if provided with a copy of the words.

(1) A Love Song

Drink to me only with thine eyes
And I will pledge with mine;
Or leave a kiss but in the cup,
And I'll not ask for wine.
The thirst that from the soul doth rise
Doth ask a gift divine,
But might I of Jove's nectar sup,
I would not change for thine.

(2) Ode To Joy

Years are coming, years are going
Creeds may change and pass away,
But the power of love is growing
Stronger, surer, day by day.
Be ye as the light of morning,
Like the beauteous dawn unfold,
With your radiant hues adorning
All the world in shades of gold.

Thaw the hearts that now are frozen,
Thaw them by the rays of love,
And the task that ye have chosen,
Will be blest all else above.
For persistent, pure devotion
To the good of humankind
Is the star of our emotion,
Is the anchor of the mind.

Selfish claims will soon no longer,
Raise their harsh discordant sounds,
For the law of love will conquer,
Bursting hatred's narrow bounds;
Human love will spread a glory
Filling us with gladsome mirth,
Songs of joy proclaim the story
Of a fair, transfigured earth.

(Words by Gustav Spiller; Music by Beethoven)

(3) A Day In Autumn

I walk the unfrequented road,
With open eye and ear,
I watch afield the farmer load,
The bounty of the year.

I filch the fruit of no man's toil —
No trespasser am I,
And yet I reap from every soil
And the unmeasured sky.

A beauty springtime never knew,
Haunts all the quiet ways,
And sweeter shines the landscape through
Its veil of autumn haze.

I face the hills, the streams, the wood,
And feel with all akin;
I ope my heart — their fortitude
And peace and joy flow in.

(Words by F.C. Hosmer; Music by T. Hawes)

If all of these suggestions for communal singing seem a bit highbrow, there are always the songs familiar to any football crowd ("You'll Never Walk Alone", "Keep Right on to the End of the Road"); or other well known songs such as "If You Were the Only Girl in the World", "We'll Gather Lilacs", "Love and Marriage" and "Tea for Two" — real slushy stuff!

Recordings of old favourites and their current counterparts are not difficult to find in any good record shop and can easily be transferred to tape. In the absence of an accompanying piano or organ, this can be played in the background, which will greatly enhance both the quality and volume of the singing, and be helpful in setting the tempo.

6 POETRY AND PROSE READINGS

As with the selection of music for the ceremony, the choice of poetry and prose passages must be left to the individuals concerned, as it is so much a question of personal taste. Couples who have no great liking for literature may well prefer a plain statement of intent without any flowery additions; others, to whom poetry is a meaningful way of expressing their feelings, will welcome the idea of including some of their favourite lines. There may even be a few couples who are happy to read a poem aloud to each other. In this event, a love poem is a highly appropriate choice and of course there is no shortage of suitable ones. But lines which celebrate marriage are very much harder to find and it is these that are needed, if the poetry is to be incorporated in the text spoken by the celebrant.

We are therefore making a few suggestions, for those who are not inclined to spend hours browsing through anthologies, and for the busy celebrant who has been asked to compose the wording of a ceremony. The quotations that follow are given in full, unless they are very easy to find. In that case references are given.

- Sir Philip Sidney *"My true love hath my heart and I have his ..."*
  (Oxford Book of English Verse)

- Christopher Marlowe *"Come live with me and be my love ..."*
  (Oxford Book of English Verse)

- Shelley *"One word is too often profaned ..."*
  (Oxford Book of English Verse)

- You Are a Part of Me

  "You are a part of me. I do not know
  By what slow chemistry you first became
  A vital fibre of my being. Go
  Beyond the rim of time or space, the same
  Inflections of your voice will sing their way
  Into the depths of my mind still. Your hair
  Will gleam as bright, the artless play
  Of word and glance, gesture and the fair

*Young fingers waving, have too deeply etched
The pattern of your soul on mine. Forget
Me quickly as a laughing picture sketched
On water, I shall never know regret
Knowing no magic ever can set free
That part of you that is a part of me."*

Frank Yerby

- Shakespeare *"Let me not to the marriage of true minds ... "*
(Sonnet CXVI. See first ceremony, page 7 of this booklet).

- *"Now you will feel no rain, for each of you ... "*
(Lines from an American Indian ceremony. See second ceremony, page 10 of this booklet).

- Anatole France *"It is not enough to love passionately; you must also love well ... "*
(see fourth ceremony, page 12)

- *"We are each a secret to the other. To know one another cannot mean to know everything about each other; it means to feel mutual affection and confidence, and to believe in one another. We must not try to force our way into the personality of another. To analyse others is a rude commencement, for there is a modesty of the soul which we must recognise just as we do that of the body. No one has a right to say to another: "Because we belong to each other as we do, I have a right to know all your thoughts." Not even a mother may treat her child in that way. All demands of this sort are foolish and unwholesome. In this matter giving is the only valuable process; it is only giving that stimulates. Impart as much as you can of your spiritual being to those who are on the road with you, and accept as something precious what comes back to you from them."*

Albert Schweitzer from "Memories of Childhood and Youth"

- *"It is for the union of you and me
that there is light in the sky
It is for the union of you and me
that the earth is decked in dusky green.
It is for the union of you and me
that night sits motionless with the world in her arms;
dawn appears opening the eastern door
with sweet murmurs in her voice.*

*The boat of hope sails along on the currents of
eternity towards that union,
flowers of the ages are being gathered together
for its welcoming ritual.*

It is for the union of you and me
that this heart of mine, in the garb of a bride,
has proceeded from birth to birth
upon the surface of this ever-turning world
to choose the beloved.''

Rabindranath Tagore

7 SOME LEGAL IMPLICATIONS OF MARRIAGE

"The most important thing about marriage is its clarity," (Clerk to a Sussex magistrates' court, July 1987).

The married state gives certain rights and protection to the husband and wife in the event of separation, divorce or the death of one partner. These are clearcut and recognised in law. But for couples whose relationship is not a registered marriage and thus holds no legal validity, there is no clearly defined guiding legislation. Although the stigma of illegitimacy has at last been removed from their children, an unmarried couple enjoy little of the protection afforded to married people. Enough thought is not often given to what their position will be if they separate or if one of them dies.

We are including some notes (based on legal advice) as we feel it important to list some of the difficulties and hardships that can arise for unmarried couples. Some of these difficulties can be avoided by careful forethought; others cannot, but are risks that the couple should be aware of. Though yours may be the perfect relationship, which can never go wrong, and yours the love that will last for ever, it is as well to think ahead and cater even for what seems unlikely or impossible.

The major trouble spots fall into two categories: those that concern property and those that deal with the custody of children.

Property

There is no statute law governing the division of property upon the separation of unmarried couples. It is essential for them to consult a solicitor so that a written agreement can be drawn up that will cater for separation; and make legally valid and up-to-date wills leaving property and possessions to each other, if this is their wish. Otherwise the estate of the partner who dies will pass to the next of kin, namely their parents or family. This is particularly unfortunate where a couple have been running a business together as well as living in a jointly owned house. It is very likely to involve the surviving partner being forced to move out of the family home. Over all these matters good legal advice is absolutely essential.

As well as making wills, there are other possible steps that can be taken in order to establish property rights for cohabitees and lessen the financial hardship when one partner dies. These are (a) taking out an insurance policy; (b) putting your dependant partner's name forward for pension rights, in the event of your death; and (c) avoiding the inheritance tax by making gifts during your lifetime. For anything left to a cohabitee, unlike a spouse, will be liable to tax. In fact it has been known for cohabitees to marry when one of them is fatally ill, simply in order to qualify for the tax exemption between husband and wife. Over pension rights there are a number of complications and again legal advice should be sought.

Children

When a married couple separate or divorce, the law attempts to deal with the custody of and access to children in as civilised and fair a way as is possible. On the separation of an unmarried couple, there is no guiding legislation. All that exists is the right of a single woman to apply to court for an order that the father contribute towards the upkeep of his child. There is no comparable right for a single man. Couples with dependant children are certainly very well advised to consider marriage or to take advice about drawing up an alternative legal framework, that will cater for any eventuality. In particular an unmarried father should understand his position over access in the event of separation.

To summarise, we recommend, with all the emphasis at our command, that those of you undertaking a long-term relationship, whether it is a legally recognised marriage or not, take legal advice so that you are fully aware of your position in law and act accordingly to protect yourselves. It is important not to rely on advice gleaned from sources that are not wholly up-to-date and well-informed, as the laws governing marriage are constantly changing and being revised. Most firms of solicitors have one of their team who specialises in matrimonial matters. Or the local Citizens' Advice Bureau is always ready to provide information; the Consumers' Association publishes guides to tax management; and the Marriage Guidance Council is also available to help.

Suggestions For Further Reading

On Humanism

Barbara Smoker: HUMANISM (Ward Lock 1973; National Secular Society 1984)

Paul Kurtz: EATING THE FORBIDDEN FRUIT — The Ethics of Humanism (Prometheus 1988)

THE HUMANIST ALTERNATIVE ed. Paul Kurtz (Rationalist Press Association 1970)

James Hemming: INDIVIDUAL MORALITY (Nelson 1969; Panther 1970)

On Marriage

MARRIAGE AND THE FAMILY, chapters on the Humanist concept of marriage and the family by Harold Blackham and Harry Stopes-Roe. (Living Faiths Series, Lutterworth Press 1985)

Erich Fromm: THE ART OF LOVING (Allen and Unwin 1985)

CLAIRE RAYNER'S MARRIAGE GUIDE (Macmillan 1984)

(The last two of these titles can be bought from the Family Planning Association Book Centre, 27-35 Mortimer St., London W1. The other four titles can be bought through the British Humanist Association, 13, Prince of Wales Terrace, London W8 5PG. Leaflets on Humanism will be sent free of charge.)

Information on the practical aspects of organising a wedding is usually available in current issues of bridal magazines, such as "Brides".

This booklet has been written and compiled by Jane Wynne Willson for the British Humanist Association. She acknowledges with gratitude the help, criticism and support throughout the enterprise of Harry Stopes-Roe and Martin Horwood. She thanks Roger Fitton and David Henson for their advice on the legal section; and Claire Rayner, Diana Rookledge, Naomi Turner, Jane and Mick Phythian and all those who made comments and suggestions on the text. Finally she thanks Helena and Mark, Ruth and Steve, and Janet and Roland for permission to reproduce the words of their wedding ceremonies; and Corliss Lamont for his American text.